Contents

P9-ARK-986

Planning: Where all good kitchens begin

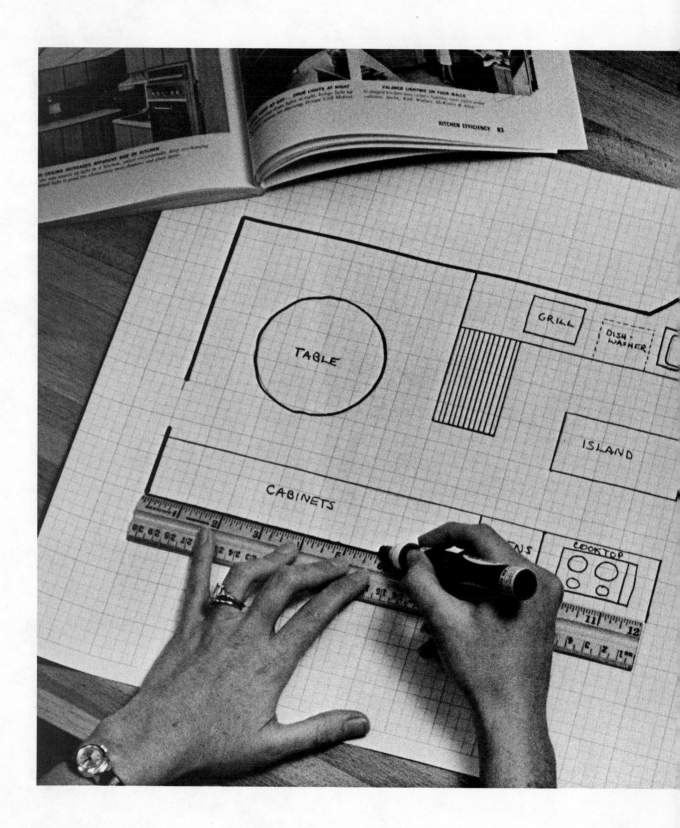

Planning & Remodeling
KITCHENS

By the Editors of Sunset Books and Sunset Magazine

LANE BOOKS · MENLO PARK, CALIFORNIA

Edited by Kathryn Arthurs

Special Consultant: Karen Hammond
Design: John Flack, JoAnn Masaoka
Artwork: Joe Seney

COVER: Neat and efficient kitchen, designed by James Flynn,
is described in more detail on page 45.
Photograph by Norman A. Plate.

Executive Editor, Sunset Books: David E. Clark

First Printing April 1974
Copyright © 1974, 1967, 1962, 1955, Lane Magazine & Book Company,
Menlo Park, California. Fourth Edition. World rights reserved. No part
of this publication may be reproduced by any mechanical, photographic,
or electronic process, or in the form of a phonographic recording, nor may
it be stored in a retrieval system, transmitted, or otherwise copied for
public or private use without prior written permission from the publisher.
Library of Congress No. 73-89582. SBN Title No. 376-01334-6.
Lithographed in the United States.

When Shakespeare wrote "To thine own self be true," he never dreamed the quote might be applied to kitchen planning. But, this application is certainly valid; your kitchen should reflect the individual needs, work habits, and entertaining style of you and your family, not those of anyone else.

To plan an efficient kitchen that will meet both your needs and your budget, you'll want to follow certain guidelines. This chapter presents these guidelines, as well as building considerations and alternatives for you to apply during your planning. Include and adapt only those ideas that will work for you. Such kitchen features as unique storage ideas and specialized working centers are pictured on pages 10-12, 20-31.

WHERE TO BEGIN?

Although the best laid plans often get changed in the shuffle of building, a thorough evaluation of the needs of both family and cook and accurate planning of all details to be included should produce a workable efficient kitchen plan. Designing the right kitchen requires careful thinking of what this room should be.

Start with an appraisal of the various family activities that depend on a functional kitchen. Does your family gather for regular meals three times a day, or do the activities of family members require an all-day smorgasbord? Do you want to eliminate family traffic in kitchen work areas during meal preparation? How frequently do you entertain? Is most entertaining formal or informal? Does more than one member of the family actively participate in the cooking? Each of these considerations and others unique to your individual situation will affect the overall kitchen plan.

A self-appraisal by the cook is the next step. Is cooking a joy or a necessary evil? Is a neat-as-a-pin appearance essential to your well-being or do open shelves and hanging utensils create a pleasant working environment? Will the cooking duties be shared? Look at your present kitchen; note your likes and dislikes regarding its efficiency and appearance. Decide which appliances with their new features will be indispensible to your new kitchen; see page 18 for appliance information to help you decide which you need and which you can do without. Look carefully at the specialty centers discussed on pages 9, 13, and 16 for possible inclusion in your plan.

Once you answer the above questions, some kitchen floor plans should be materializing. The actual floor plan begins with decisions on the basic kitchen layout to be used, the position of the work triangle (this is the triangle formed by the placement of the sink, refrigerator, and stove; see page 7), and the specialized work centers to be incorporated.

BASIC KITCHEN FLOOR PLANS

There are five main types of kitchen layouts: 1) a strip or one-wall kitchen; 2) a pullman or two-wall kitchen; 3) an L-shaped kitchen; 4) a U-shaped kitchen; 5) a kitchen with an island. Each of these kitchen floor plans presents both advantages and disadvantages to the user.

The strip or one-wall kitchen (commonly used in small-space situations such as apartments or vacation cabins), positions all appliances and work areas along one wall. The main disadvantage is the distance between the work areas; a strip kitchen does not allow a work triangle. (Work triangles are discussed on page 7.)

A pullman or two-wall kitchen divides appliances and work areas between two parallel walls. This arrangement creates a work triangle and usually provides more counter space. Its main disadvantage is that the corridor between the two walls encourages foot traffic. If the corridor leads to the outside, it may develop into a family freeway.

An L-shaped kitchen divides appliances and counter space between two walls that meet at right angles (see diagram below). Another version of this layout extends the base of the L into the room. This plan frees floor space for other uses and directs traffic away from the cook's work area. But placing appliances can create a problem. If the sink, refrigerator, and cooktop are too far apart, the working triangle will be exhausting. Every meal would require a cook with the endurance of a long-distance runner.

The U-shaped kitchen, considered by many experts to be the most efficient floor plan, divides appliances and work areas between three connected walls arranged in a U configuration (see diagram below). One leg of the U may extend into the room without wall support. Generally, the sink is placed at the base of the U, with the stove or cooktop and refrigerator installed on the facing legs. This creates a tight work triangle that eliminates wasted effort. Traffic patterns form naturally outside the work area. Counter space is continuous, and ample storage is made available. Disadvantages arise only if the kitchen area is too small.

Island kitchens have helped expand these basic floor plans in recent years. All layouts except the pullman kitchen can benefit from the addition of an island. The

SIX BASIC FLOOR PLANS are shown below. Each plan includes three main appliances and shows possible placement.

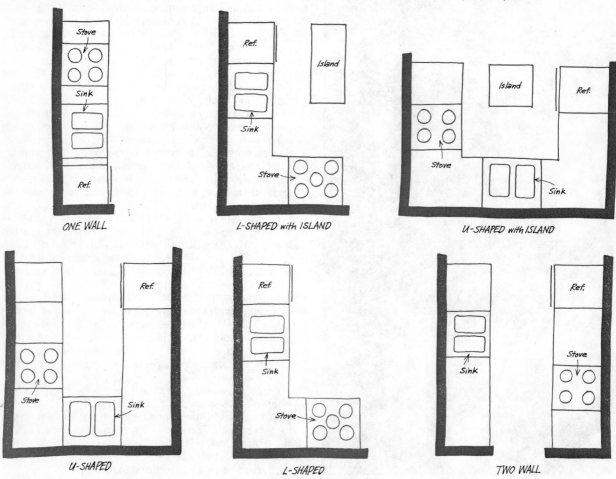

ONE WALL   L-SHAPED with ISLAND   U-SHAPED with ISLAND

U-SHAPED   L-SHAPED   TWO WALL

island is free-standing and usually centrally located; it can be mobile, adding extra work space wherever needed. It may contain a sink or cooktop, or may augment counter space. Islands efficiently control traffic, provide a tighter work triangle, create more work space, and usually add more storage. They can also provide an eating counter. Islands are especially useful in defining large kitchen spaces into functional work areas. Examples of island kitchens are illustrated by diagrams below.

THE WORK TRIANGLE

Appliance placement is the first consideration after the kitchen layout is determined. The three main appliances —sink, refrigerator, and stove or cooktop—should form a triangle whose sides total no less than 12 feet and no more than 22 feet. This is called the work triangle. (If ovens and cooktop are separate units, the ovens may be located outside the triangle.)

A work triangle of this size allows for enough counter and storage space so work isn't cramped, yet arranges appliances and their related centers (see pages 7-8) so the cook won't cover great distances during meal preparation.

KITCHEN CENTERS

The military strategy of divide and conquer can be utilized by the kitchen planner. By dividing space into specialized work areas, the related tasks become easier to perform, and the final outcome is an efficient functional kitchen—a sure victory for the designer and the cook.

Basic centers

Since each kitchen task requires a particular working surface and/or appliance, specialized tools, and necessary ingredients, it makes good sense to organize centers by locating the needed equipment with the appliances in an adequate work area.

Four centers are basic to most kitchens: a refrigerator center; a preparation or mix center; a stove center; and

THE WORK TRIANGLE is illustrated in basic floor plans. (The one-wall plan doesn't allow a triangle.)

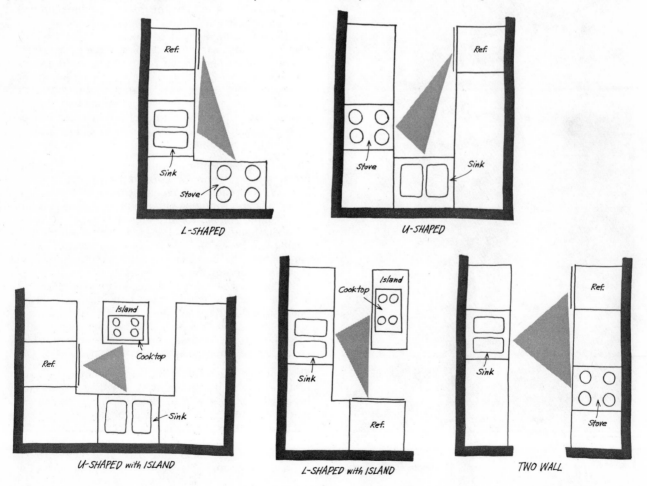

L-SHAPED

U-SHAPED

U-SHAPED with ISLAND

L-SHAPED with ISLAND

TWO WALL

HEAT-RESISTANT TILES in countertop create patterned landing pad beside the stove. Design: Michael Moreland.

SHELF UNDER COOKTOP pulls out to hold hot dishes and pans from ovens or cooktop. Architect: J. Lloyd Conrich.

PULL-OUT BOARD becomes a countertop for isolated wall oven, disappearing when not in use. Architect: Walter Eagle.

a sink or cleanup center. Other more specialized centers such as a baking or serving center can increase kitchen efficiency.

The refrigerator center handles the storage of perishable foodstuffs. A refrigerator/freezer combination or a separate freezer unit allows longer storage of many foods. (An infrequently used freezer may best be located in an adjacent utility room or in the garage, freeing valuable kitchen space.) Pantry space for foodstuffs not requiring refrigeration is also necessary. A counter approximately 1½ feet wide located on the door latch side of the refrigerator serves as a landing pad for groceries to be stored inside and items to be taken out for food preparation. Ideally, this center should be located near the preparation center.

The preparation center provides an area for mixing and preparing foods prior to cooking or serving them. A 3 to 3½-foot counter is recommended, with a surface for cutting and chopping either built-in or readily available. Ample storage for dry ingredients, baking pans, casseroles, and any utensils needed for measuring and mixing will be helpful. Good knife storage can be incorporated. The best place for this center is near the refrigerator and/or the sink center.

Storage can create a problem in this center. Small appliances used in food preparation, such as a mixer, blender, and can opener, need carefully planned storage. If these appliances aren't handy, you may not make the effort to use them. If counter space isn't available, an appliance garage may be the answer.

The stove center controls cooking. It contains a stove or a cooktop with separate ovens. (Separate ovens may be located anywhere in the kitchen, but generally are placed near the cooktop.) Place a counter at least 2 feet wide beside the stove, with an adjacent landing surface of heat-proof material, either portable or built-in, to accommodate hot pots and pans (see above, left). Supply storage for skillets and pans to be used on the stove. Spoons and other implements used during cooking should also be stored nearby. If ovens are separated from the cooktop, provide a heat-proof surface for hot dishes coming from the oven.

The sink center handles food washing and trimming, dish cleanup, and garbage disposal. Appliances include a double-bowl sink, a mechanical garbage disposer, and a dishwasher. A trash compactor would also be placed nearby. Counters are needed on both sides of the sink: one 3 feet wide on the right side for stacking dirty dishes and one 2½ feet wide on the left side for draining dishes. A dishwasher is commonly placed to the left of the sink. (A left-handed person may prefer it positioned to the right of the sink.) Provide storage for soap and other cleaning materials and towels near the sink. Locate dish and flatware storage close to the dishwasher for easy unloading.

Combination centers

If your kitchen space is limited, combining basic work centers may solve the problem. In combination, two basic centers share the use of one counter. To determine the needed counter size, find the widest counter of the two centers and then add one foot to it. The resulting counter allows both centers to function at the same time.

For example, consider combining the refrigerator center and the preparation center. The counter requirement for the refrigerator center is 1½ feet, for the preparation center, 3½ feet. Take the widest counter—the preparation center at 3½ feet—and add one foot to it; a counter 4½ feet wide results.

A word of caution: the kitchen designers and researchers who developed the above formula insist that no kitchen should contain less than 10 lineal feet of full-use base cabinets. Don't economize so much on the counters that needed base cabinets will be eliminated.

Specialty centers

In addition to the basic centers described above, specialty centers can add new dimensions to your kitchen. Depending on your specific needs and available space, consider incorporating one or more of these centers into your kitchen plan. Keep in mind that these centers are functional only if the tasks to be performed in them will be frequently repeated.

The most common specialty centers are a baking center, a beverage bar, a serving or buffet center, a family eating area, an office center, and a barbecue center. As in the basic centers, necessary working surfaces, equipment and appliances to be utilized, and adequate working space to perform specific tasks are organized into one area.

A baking center is a boon to the cook who specializes in homemade breads and fancy pastries. Most bakers prefer a work surface of wood, formica, or marble for rolling out and/or kneading dough. (You may wish to lower this counter to a better working level. Many cooks prefer a 32-inch counter for stirring and chop-

ping. For further information on counter heights, see page 17.) If a special working surface can't be built into the counter, consider a pull-out board either of wood or coated with marble. Sufficient storage for mixers and other appliances, mixing bowls, measuring spoons and cups, and other pertinent equipment should be nearby. You'll need storage space for flour, sugar, spices, and other ingredients used in baking. One handy solution to storing cumbersome items, such as flour and sugar, is tin-lined drawers; large amounts of these frequently used staples can be safely kept.

If you own a heavy-duty mixer, you may want to install it on a special shelf that swings up into place while the mixer is in use, then retreats into a cabinet for storage. This principle is similar to that of a typing stand (see below).

Several types of baking centers are pictured on pages 10-11.

A beverage bar is handy both for parties and to route constant water drinkers away from kitchen work areas. If sodas, splits, shakes, and sundaes are your forte, the bar converts easily to a soda fountain. Ample glass and

(Continued on page 13)

SWING-UP SHELF holds a heavy-duty mixer; shelf makes a sturdy work surface for bulky appliance. Design: Janean.

Baking centers

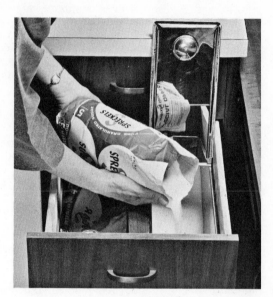

METAL BINS fit into drawer, are used to store sugar, flour, and other staples.

SMALL SPACE CENTER (above) contains marble insert for pastry and candy making, built-in flour sifter. Ovens, storage for ingredients and utensils are close at hand. Architect: Richard Perkins. **Right:** Self-contained center has small appliance area with strip outlets, marble insert, ample storage for baking equipment. Design: John Scaduto, Mayta and Jensen.

BAKING AREA has appliance storage with strip outlets, spice storage, metal-lined drawers for flour, sugar. Architect: Otto Poticha.

LOWERED COUNTER is good height (32 inches) for stirring, rolling out pastry, has laminated maple working surface. Design: Janean.

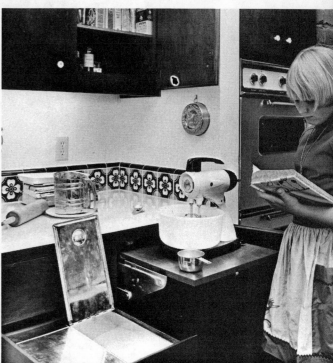

MIXER on swing-up stand, metal-lined drawers for flour are part of baking center. Architect: James T. Flynn.

Serving counters

PULL-OUT BUFFET (top right) on metal drawer slides hides in wall. **Bottom right:** Extended, counter holds a variety of dishes. Architect: Donald Gibbs.

TILED COUNTER (left) contains food warmer, ample storage for dishes, flatware. Location is near dining area, out of kitchen work area. Architect: Don McKee. **Above:** Ten-foot counter runs length of dining area, contains storage for dishes, linens. Architect: Theodore Milhous.

(Continued from page 9)

bottle storage is essential to this center. A second sink is helpful but not necessary. If the refrigerator is at a distance, ice storage would be convenient, or you might want to consider installing a second refrigerator. If you like to keep a large supply of wine on hand, include wine racks in this area.

A serving or buffet center takes the work out of meal serving. A well-planned area allows table setting, food service, and cleanup without frequent trips between kitchen and dining room, patio, or other eating areas. Ideally, you would situate this center near dish and flatware storage and the cooktop and ovens. Quick and easy serving can be accomplished by a buffet counter, a pass-through into the dining room or to the patio, or a mobile serving cart. A combination of these could also be beneficial; a pass-through to the patio area and a serving cart to be wheeled into the dining room handles both areas efficiently.

A kitchen counter located out of major kitchen work areas, either with a heat-proof surface (such as tile) or portable pads for holding hot dishes, permits easy buffet-type service. This method works equally well for family meals and large parties. Consider the traffic problems involved; people should move along the counter and then to the table without any congestion. An eating counter located out of the work triangle can also double as a buffet counter.

Another possibility for easy meal serving is a pass-through. A pass-through is a hole in the wall, with or without a door, above counter space for handing dishes, flatware, linens, and food containers from one area to another. Pass-throughs work equally well from the kitchen to the dining room or to patio or pool areas. Unlike the buffet counter, this center doesn't take room away from valuable kitchen space.

A mobile serving cart presents still another possibility. Dishes, flatware, and the meal itself can be loaded onto the cart, wheeled to the table, and reloaded as after-dinner debris for the return trip. A cart is especially functional if dish storage and cooking facilities are at opposite ends of the kitchen; the cart can be wheeled to various storage areas and work centers for easy loading.

Storing the cart when not in use is also an easy matter. A garage that the cart rolls into neatly conceals it. If the cart has a working surface, such as a butcher block top, a parking spot at the end of a counter will add extra working space to the kitchen. Both of these options are pictured on pages 14-15.

A family eating area in the kitchen takes much of the effort out of day-to-day informal dining. It also provides a pleasant area for after school or summertime snacking—even for a midmorning coffee klatch with a neighbor. The two most common eating surfaces found in kitchens are a counter or a table. Be sure to allow a surface space of 24 inches by 24 inches for each diner. Chairs or stools need approximately 42 inches maneuvering room. Refrigerator or other appliance doors should not open into the eating area.

An office center in the kitchen enables the cook to plan menus, organize grocery lists, and handle bills and cor-

(Continued on page 16)

PATIO PASS-THROUGH is perfect for outdoor entertaining. Shelves below hold serving needs. Architect: Richard Perkins.

KITCHEN-TO-DINING ROOM pass-through has bifold doors to hide opening. Architects: Allen D. Fong, George Mock.

Mobile serving carts

LADEN WITH DISHES, cart is ready for table setting. Design: Harper Poulson.

MARBLE-TOPPED CART adds working space to this kitchen island. Architect: Marvin Witt, Jr.

*WOODEN CART (right) is loaded with dishes, food to enter dining room, returns after meal with dirty dishes. **Above:** Cart was commercially made; island was designed to store it. Architect: Otto Poticha.*

CART (left) is topped with wooden cutting board for chopping, cutting tasks; it rolls wherever surface is needed. Design: Mrs. Norman D. Louis. **Below:** Movable butcher's block adds extra counter space to kitchen. Design: E. J. Freck.

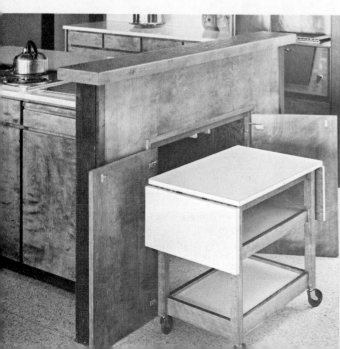

SERVING CART disappears into kitchen island when not in use. Flip-up extensions add extra surface to cart top which doubles as counter space. Architect: A. O. Bumgardner and Partners.

OFFICE for menu planning and correspondence is outside the kitchen work area. Architect: John R. Peterson.

BUILT-IN CENTER for kitchen planning has working surface, open shelves. Design: Sabin O'Neal Mitchell.

(Continued from page 13)

respondence. A writing surface and a chair are essential. Space for cook books, writing supplies, a telephone, and possibly a typewriter should be provided. Two examples are shown above.

A barbecue center that organizes the various paraphernalia used into one area benefits the family that loves barbecued food. If you barbecue on a patio or by a pool area, plan a nearby storage cabinet for fuel, long-handled utensils, and other necessary items.

Special barbecue grills are available for kitchen installation; they permit barbecuing to be moved indoors for year-round enjoyment. Used in conjunction with a ventilating hood or fan, these grills simulate the effect of meat barbecued over hot coals. One grill incorporates the fan into the counter unit, freeing space overhead. These grills are usually located near the stove center, with necessary equipment stored nearby.

If you have an indoor, built-in barbecue that uses live coals, good ventilation is essential; charcoal fumes can be noxious.

BUILDING YOUR KITCHEN

Once the kitchen plan is drawn up, consider the details that will be involved in the actual building. What type of countertop will serve you best? Which wall and floor coverings are most functional? What is the best height for your counters? Should you consider buying new appliances? How much lighting and ventilation is needed? The following section offers product information and guidelines to aid you in making decisions.

Materials for kitchen surfaces

The kitchen is perhaps cleaned more frequently and more thoroughly than any other room in a house, the bathroom being the only contender to this title. So ease of cleaning and durability should be major factors in choosing the various building materials to be used in your new or remodeled kitchen. Surfaces receiving the most wear are countertops, floors, and walls.

Be sure to consider an architect's or contractor's suggestions about building materials (if you're using professional help). Since these professionals work constantly with building materials, they see and evaluate a product's advantages and weaknesses. They are also aware of any innovative products.

Countertops offer the widest selection of possible materials. Ceramic tile and plastic laminate are the most common; wooden butcher block, brushed steel, and marble are other possibilities. Special inserts add versatility to any type of counter. The ideal kitchen incorporates a combination of these counter types, since different kitchen tasks require specialized surfaces.

Ceramic tile is available in a wide selection of colors and patterns; try staining grout for color contrast and easier upkeep. The tile surface accepts hot pots and pans and cutting or chopping. It is non-absorbent, resistant to scratches and stains, and easy to clean. Initial installation is expensive, but tile is more durable than most other surfaces.

Plastic laminate is a common counter material, easy to clean and inexpensive to install. It is available in many colors, and the wide selection of patterns includes simulated marble, brick, and wood grain. Extreme heat can cause it to burn, and it can be cut or stained if used abusively.

Wooden, butcher block counters add warmth and interest to kitchens. The surface is perfect for cutting, chopping, and making pastry. It is expensive to install; it will burn, cut, and stain; and it will probably need occasional sanding and refinishing.

Metal countertops are useful as inserts near stove or oven units for holding hot pots and pans. Initial installation is expensive. The surface cuts and scratches easily; the brushed steel camouflages minor abuse.

Marble is the most expensive counter material. Its beautiful veined surface is impervious to water and heat. If not treated properly, it will stain, crack, and scratch. It is best used as a small insert for pastry and candy making or as a heat-proof landing pad near the stove or ovens. Synthetic marble is also available but chiefly for use in bathrooms.

Combining counter surfaces creates a more functional kitchen. A wooden butcher block or glass-ceramic insert aids in cutting and chopping foods. A heat-proof pad of metal, tile, glass-ceramic material or marble serves as a landing pad for hot pans and pots. Butcher block or marble inserts double as pastry boards. For greatest efficiency, these counter inserts should be placed as near as possible to the kitchen center they are to serve. Look for further information on kitchen centers on pages 7-9.

Flooring materials most commonly used in kitchens are resilient floor coverings and kitchen carpeting. If properly chosen, both surfaces will serve well.

Resilient floor coverings come in many forms: linoleum; asphalt tile; vinyl tile; cork tile; sheet vinyl; or floorings that combine some of these materials. The newer inlaid sheet vinyls are available with no-wax surfaces—a true timesaver. The home handyman can lay some of these floorings; others require professional installation. Base your decision on the type of resilient flooring that will best serve you. The variables are cost of materials and installation, durability of materials, and variety of available colors and patterns.

Carpeting in the kitchen is a recent innovation. It is a soft, quiet, warm material, available in many colors and patterns. It comes either as wall-to-wall carpeting or carpet tiles; the tiles don't require professional installation. Choose a short, non-sculptured carpet that is durable and stain-resistant. Carpeting is generally more expensive than resilient flooring.

Wall coverings used in the kitchen are usually paint or wallpaper. Both provide durable surfaces and, for a quick kitchen face lift, can be changed with relative ease.

Paint is inexpensive, easy for the homeowner to apply, and available in all colors of the rainbow. Choose washable paint for an easy-to-clean surface.

Wallpaper comes in a wide variety of colors and patterns. Cost varies, depending on your choice. Most wallpapers can be hung by an amateur. Be sure the wallpaper you choose is scrubbable.

Choosing cabinets

The main decision regarding new kitchen cabinets is whether to use prefabricated or stock cabinets, or whether to have them custom built by a cabinetmaker. Both cabinet types come in a variety of materials, styles, and finishes. Inspect both types before making your decision; cabinets represent a large investment.

Custom-built cabinets offer the greatest freedom, since they can be constructed to exact specifications. Cabinetmakers usually offer a wide variety of finishes and cabinet styles. Be sure to get several bids and ask for references from previous customers.

Prefabricated or stock cabinets come in a wide variety of materials, styles, and finishes. They can be constructed of metal, wood, plastic laminate, or a combination of materials.

Since they are stock, cabinet sizes have been standardized. Base cabinets are commonly 24 inches deep and 34 inches high (with a 2-inch countertop, bringing it to the standard 36-inch height). Wall cabinets are generally 12 inches deep and from 12 to 36 inches high. Cabinet widths normally start at 9 inches and go to 36 inches in increments of 3 inches. Fillers are used to finish off an odd-sized counter. Some prefabricated cabinet companies allow custom designed cabinets to be special ordered; this will add to the expense.

With the standardized wall cabinets, there will be extra space between the top of the units and the ceiling. This space can be enclosed for extra storage, be used for lighting fixtures, or be left open.

Exact measurements are essential. Always have your final measurements checked by the company before ordering stock cabinets.

Unless you are a skilled woodworker, it is best to leave cabinet installation to the experts.

Counter heights

Choosing the proper counter height is essential to the well-being of the cook. A 36-inch counter height is considered average. Drop-in appliance manufacturers and stock prefabricated cabinetmakers use this height as a guideline. Built-in dishwashers and drop-in stoves require at least a 36-inch high counter.

The short cook may prefer a counter height of 34 inches or less. Lowering one counter or an island for ease in chopping and stirring can alleviate the problem; a separate cooktop unit can be placed in a lowered counter. Reduce prefabricated cabinets by shortening the kick space at the bottom. Built-in dishwashers and drop-in stoves will still need a 36-inch counter.

The tall cook may wish to raise counters a few inches. Again, one working surface higher than the standard 36 inches may be sufficient. If most surfaces are raised, also raise upper wall cabinets to keep the kitchen in proportion.

Keep resale value of your home in mind whenever a kitchen is altered from the norm. Low counters of 32 inches or high ones of 39 inches may severely limit the number of prospective buyers in the future.

Choosing appliances

Kitchen appliances have recently undergone a metamorphosis. The utilitarian ugly ducklings of the past have become swans, both in form and function. Even appliances purchased a few years ago are dated. Consider new appliances for your custom kitchen or remodel; their timesaving devices and new features (see below) may be well worth the extra expense.

Size and working requirements of new appliances may dictate their placement. Check your kitchen measurements carefully and be aware of special appliance operation needs so these appliances can be included in your final layout.

Most new appliances come with literature regarding their use and care. Be sure to read the information carefully, following all directions and suggestions to prolong the life and insure the efficiency of your new appliance.

Stoves and separate cooktop and oven units have recently revolutionized cooking. Burners can be gas or electric-powered; smooth-top cooking units powered by electricity utilize a new glass/ceramic surface that dramatically simplifies cleaning up spilled food. With the new self-cleaning ovens, you can forget ammonia fumes and broken fingernails.

Two types of oven cleaning systems are available both in stoves and wall oven units: self-cleaning (or pyrolitic) and continuous-cleaning. The self-cleaning system uses a separate, timed, high-temperature cycle to burn off residue. The continuous-cleaning system cleans as the oven bakes at normal temperatures. Large spillovers must still be removed manually in the continuous-cleaning system.

Other optional features include removable stove and oven parts for easy cleaning, food warmers, and oven timers. Cooktop options are barbecue grills, griddles, and rotisseries. One unit contains a built-in fan that eliminates the need for overhead ventilation. For further information on kitchen ventilation, see page 19.

Refrigerators and refrigerator/freezer combinations feature self-defrosting models in addition to the standard manual defrost. This option is a definite timesaver. For keeping meats and fresh produce, special compartments are available, some with individual temperature controls. Many models contain adjustable shelves for more efficient storage. Ice makers and cold water dispensers are new convenience features, but keep in mind that they require a water line.

A single-door refrigerator usually contains a frozen food compartment; these compartments are not for long-term freezer storage. In refrigerator/freezer combinations, each unit has an individual door; they can be side-by-side models or ones in which the freezer is located at the top or bottom. Doors can be hinged from either side to fit your kitchen layout.

Kitchen sinks are in constant use, from initial food preparation to final meal cleanup. Analyze your needs, choosing a sink accordingly.

Sinks can be constructed either of stainless steel or of cast iron or steel coated with porcelain. Porcelain sinks come finished in white or in a variety of colors. Stainless steel sinks generally have a brushed surface that camouflages scratches and wear marks.

Single, double, and triple-bowl sinks are available. Consider a single-bowl sink only if you have a dishwasher. A triple-bowl sink permits more than one cook to work at the same time.

A garbage disposer can be installed in all sink types. A shallow bowl containing the disposer is an option for a double-bowl sink and is the standard center sink in a triple-bowl unit.

New sink options feature dispensers for liquid soap, hand lotion, and instant hot water.

Dishwashers are the biggest timesavers in any modern kitchen. Models come built-in or portable, top or front-loading. Some contain soft food disposers that eliminate careful prerinsing. Most models provide adjustable shelves for easy loading. More expensive models have a variety of cycles that handle cleaning jobs from extra dirty pots and pans to fragile china and crystal.

Garbage disposers grind up most soft food wastes. Many models are sturdy enough to handle such tough garbage as fruit pits, celery, and corn husks. The two main types of disposers are batch-feed and continuous-feed. The continuous-feed disposer allows you to add scraps as the unit is grinding. The batch-feed disposes of one load at a time. As a precautionary measure, be sure the on/off switch is out of a child's reach.

Trash compactors are newcomers to the kitchen. A recent innovation, they reduce normal, dry household waste to a fraction of its normal size, cutting down on garbage volume. (This appliance does not replace a garbage disposer; it is best to avoid placing wet garbage in a compactor.) If you have a large family or more than average amounts of garbage, consider including a compactor in your kitchen planning.

Microwave ovens, like compactors, are relatively new kitchen appliances. For busy families who eat on the run or at several different times, meals cooked in microwave ovens can be prepared in minutes. Whether you cook for one person or a dozen, a microwave oven will save time.

The cooking principle of a microwave oven is totally different from that of a conventional oven. Cooking is achieved through electromagnetic waves generated from a magnetron tube. These waves are either reflected, transmitted, or absorbed. Metals reflect them; glass, paper, and most plastics transmit them; food absorbs them. Microwaves enter food and cause its moisture molecules to vibrate rapidly; the friction created results in heat energy that cooks the food. Utensils to cook in can be almost anything but metal—even a paper plate!

Microwave ovens can be portable, countertop models, built-in units, or part of a freestanding stove unit. Some of the latter contain two ovens, one of which is microwave, one conventional.

Because of possibly dangerous leakage of microwaves, all microwave ovens must meet stringent safety requirements. Ovens need at least two separate interlocks to shut off energy whenever the door is opened. Special door construction must keep radiant energy leakage to a level considered negligible.

Although microwave cooking does have limitations (foods such as steak or chops will not brown) and will not replace your conventional oven, it does thaw frozen foods, heat leftovers, and cook a wide variety of foods in a short time.

Lighting the kitchen

Good kitchen lighting depends on illuminating the kitchen as a whole and spotlighting specific work areas. Proper lighting allows meal preparation and cleanup without causing eyestrain.

Overall lighting should provide glare-free, shadowless light on all floor areas and traffic paths. It should permit easy cleaning and safe passage through the kitchen. Common fixtures for general lighting are individual ceiling units or large ceiling panels, both of a translucent material, or a skylight for natural light. (A skylight will require additional general lighting.)

The color of the kitchen will also affect the overall lighting; white and light-toned colors reflect light, whereas darker colors tend to absorb it. A kitchen in dark wood-tones requires more general lighting than a pale yellow room.

You can focus light on specific work areas in a number of ways: incandescent or fluorescent lighting under cabinets; spotlights on the ceiling or under a soffit; light units in a hood; individual fixtures positioned over a major work area, such as the sink. Fluorescent lighting with warm-toned tubes is best for kitchen use.

If you plan to add a number of new light fixtures, have wiring checked to be sure your present electrical system is adequate.

Ventilating the kitchen

Nothing can be worse than the cooking odors of last night's liver. Good ventilation removes unpleasant odors, steam, liquefied fat particles, and excessive heat, all the necessary evils that cooking creates.

Locate exhaust fans as near to the stove or cooktop as possible for greatest efficiency. One cooktop unit incorporates a fan right on the burner unit. A ceiling fan must be powerful enough to draw up odors, heat, and grease. Because a hood fan is closer to the cooking, it will be more effective with less power.

Ducting the exhaust out of the house can be tricky, especially if your stove or cooktop is located on an interior wall or on an island. For best results, consult your architect, contractor, or a ventilation specialist.

Planning storage

Proper storage in the kitchen is essential. Without adequate, usable storage areas, many items will be misplaced or seldom used, causing a corresponding drop in kitchen efficiency. Specific storage in kitchen centers is discussed on pages 7-9, 13, 15. Additional types of specialized storage are shown on the next 12 pages.

Present storage areas can be implemented with commercially available units. Standard-size drawers, bins, shelves, turntables, and special racks can be found in Housewares sections of department or hardware stores. These units can store hard-to-place items like pan lids, spice jars, and prepared foods.

Frequently used items—pots and pans, table linens, spices and herbs, canned goods and packaged foodstuffs, small appliances, and garbage containers—need specialized storage that is easily accessible. Several ideas for storing each of these items are pictured on pages 20-31; perhaps you can adapt some of these suggestions in your own kitchen planning.

PREPARING FOR CONSTRUCTION

Finally, make the decision on how best to accomplish the actual kitchen construction. Should you hire an architect or a kitchen designer to plan and draw up the detailed plans or do all the planning and drafting yourself? Should you use a contractor? How much of the work, if any, should you do yourself? These decisions will greatly affect the planning, cost, and timetable of your new or remodeled kitchen.

If construction or remodeling will be extensive, carefully consider the services offered by an architect or kitchen designer. Their experience in kitchen planning and building procedures can prevent expensive errors. You can hire them only to prepare detailed blueprints of the kitchen or give them the authority to supervise the entire job. To find a good architect or designer, rely on personal recommendations. Most architects and kitchen designers are listed in the yellow pages of your local telephone book. It's always wise to get several bids and ask for references from former clients.

If you decide to design the kitchen yourself, you'll need to provide a detailed blueprint for the contractor and/or workmen. It is advisable to consult with an architect about your final drawings to avoid costly changes during construction.

If you hire a contractor to oversee kitchen construction, ask several contractors for competitive bids. The bidding should be based on detailed, approved plans. Don't hesitate to ask contractors for references. Whenever possible, examine their workmanship for former clients.

If you wish to do part or all of the job yourself, be sure you are well qualifed for the various tasks. Most remodeling projects will have to pass local building codes. Some jobs, such as laying floor tiles, hanging wallpaper, and painting walls and cabinets, are easy for the average handyman. Others, such as plumbing, electrical work, and cabinet construction, are best left to skilled workmen.

Storing cooking utensils

VERTICAL DIVIDERS store baking pans, large serving trays; all items are visible. Architect: Don L. McKee.

DRAWERS (right) below cooktop hold pots, pans, casseroles. **Above:** Cooking utensils hang from wrought iron rack attached to ceiling. Items are handy, decorative. Design: C. E. Rosebrooks.

PERFORATED HARDBOARD DIVIDERS *hold platters, serving trays, utensils on hooks. Panels slide out for easy selection. Design: Mayta and Jensen.*

MAGNETIC STRIPS *hold knives, spoons, other small utensils. Architect: Robert C. Peterson.*

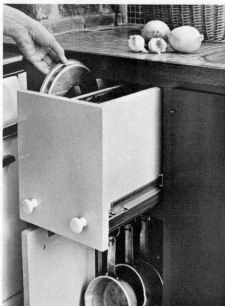

PULL-OUT RACK *(far left) holds cooking pots, pans; unit is available commercially.* **Left:** *Drawer above rack especially designed to store pot lids. Architect: James A. Jennings.*

Storing table linens

LARGE WOODEN DOWELS (left) attached to metal drawer slides pull out to choose tablecloths. Architect: Loren D. Durr. **Right:** Built-in buffet has drawers to hold placemats, napkins, linens. Architect: Warren C. Heylman.

SEE-THROUGH STORAGE (right) is accessible from dining room or kitchen. Architect: Richard Sundeleaf.
Above: Under counter storage has pull-out shelves for linens. Design: The Richardson Associates.

DRAWERS facing dining area keep linens, placemats close at hand. Patterned napkins are folded and ready to use. Design: Janean.

TABLECLOTHS hang on wood hangers in dining room storage area. Architects: Payne, Settecase.

PLASTIC RODS (left) are hollow, are held in place by wooden pegs attached to chains. Round shape of rod keeps pressed linens from creasing.
Above: Tablecloths can be removed by pulling out wooden peg.

Storing spices

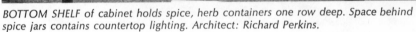

BOTTOM SHELF of cabinet holds spice, herb containers one row deep. Space behind spice jars contains countertop lighting. Architect: Richard Perkins.

SHALLOW SPACE (above) in front of cooktop unit can store spice jars. Small pull-out shelf utilizes additional space for small container storage. **Right:** Stair-step shelves hold spice, herb containers so that all labels are visible at a glance.

STORAGE CABINET *pulls out; supports are metal drawer slides.* **Center** *divider keeps containers one row deep. Design: E. J. Frech.*

UNUSED SPACE *adjacent to wall ovens becomes spice storage. Architect: Leonard Veitzer.*

SMALL WALL AREA *(left) between tiled backsplash, pass-through is perfect for spice storage.* **Above:** *Extra shelf under overhead cabinets has swing-up door for selecting spices. Design: Leroy Devereux.*

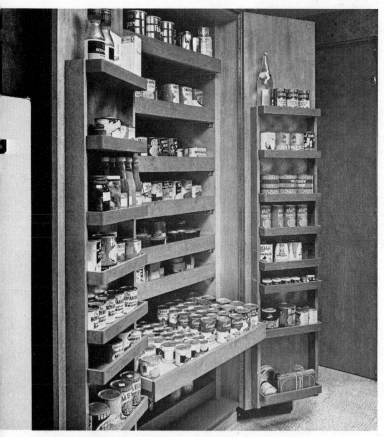

FLOOR-TO-CEILING CLOSET contains pantry. Drawers pull out, so contents are visible. Architect: Stanley Jacobson.

CUT-OUT SHELVES in walk-in pantry allow storage one item deep for easy selection. Design: Charles L. Larson.

WALL CABINETS store canned goods, packaged foods. Racks on doors hold spices, herbs. Architect: Moritz Kundig.

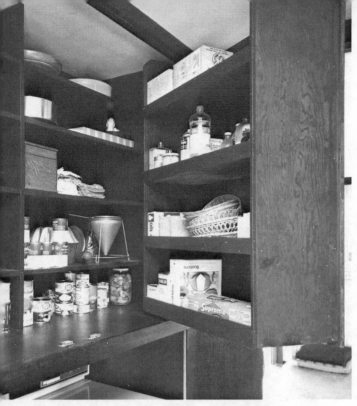

OVERHEAD CABINETS (left) in laundry area contain pantry items, extra kitchen utensils. Architect: Charles Metcalf.
Right: *Slanted shelves hold canned goods; remove one, the rest roll forward. Architect: Earl Kai Chann.*

PANTRY (left) has adjustable shelves.
Architect: A. Jane Duncombe, Duncombe-
Roland-Miller. **Above:** *Pull-out drawers
hold canned goods, prepared foods.*

STORAGE SPACE at end of eating counter is good for small appliances, other items. Door pulls up to open.

TOASTER is handy, has electric outlet in cabinet to keep it ready to use. Architects: Bull, Field, Volkmann, Stockwell.

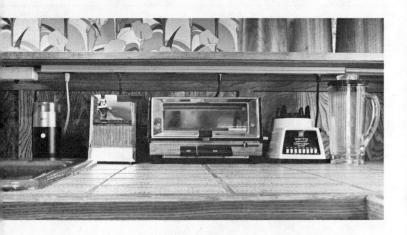

OPEN NICHE (above) under counter overhang has strip electrical outlets so each appliance has a plug. Appliances are placed on countertop to use. **Right:** Appliance storage has tambour door (as on a roll-top desk), pulls down to hide contents. Architects: Robert C. Peterson, Victor K. Thompson.

COUNTERTOP CABINET has sliding platform for toaster oven. Electrical outlet is at the back of the cabinet.

APPLIANCES PULL FORWARD on trays outfitted with nylon rollers, hide behind bifold doors when not in use.

STORAGE FOR APPLIANCES, small condiments uses space above the counter in the corner of a U-shaped kitchen. Design: Janean.

Garbage disposal

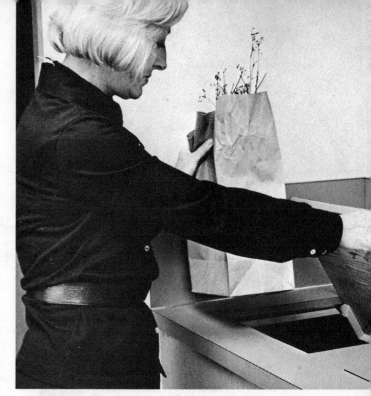

CUT-OUT LIDS in countertop help in sorting the garbage for recycling. Each opening has a container below to catch refuse.

ROUND CUTTING BOARD conceals countertop opening to garbage container. Architect: Jacob Robbins.

DOOR in tiled wall opens into metal garbage chute. Architects: Donald James Clark, Thomas Higley.

DRAWER under cutting board holds plastic garbage basket. Architect: Marvin Witt, Jr.

TIP-OUT DRAWER under sink holds commercial plastic container; can be removed to empty refuse.

TWIN CONTAINERS (above) are for recycling garbage. Containers can be emptied individually. **Left:** Cutting board is behind garbage opening for food scraps. Architect: Mark Mills.

Remodeling: A collection of idea-filled kitchens

Whether your kitchen remodeling plans are simple or extensive, you'll find new ideas from seeing how other home owners or architects have solved common kitchen problems. Often their solutions will suggest ways you can remodel to improve your own kitchen work area. It's unlikely you'll find your exact floor plan represented, but you can adapt many of the ideas to fit your individual situation.

This chapter presents 35 remodeled kitchens. The kitchen layouts, styles, and family needs pictured are very diverse, offering dozens of interesting methods for improving the appearance and efficiency of your kitchen. Many kitchen floor plans are included to help you visualize the work areas and their orientation to surrounding rooms.

One example of the major transformation you can achieve through kitchen remodeling is illustrated by the photos on these two pages. The "Before" photo shows the situation that faced the owners and architect. The "After" photograph demonstrates how they solved the problems. Careful planning should create an updated, efficient kitchen reflecting the owner's needs and personality. For further information on the kitchen pictured here, see pages 66-67.

AFTER   BEFORE

Kitchen designed for entertaining

This is a kitchen for people who enjoy entertaining. Its design is functional for a single cook, yet there's enough room if extra helpers are needed.

The long laminated-wood counters provide a good working surface for cutting, chopping, and making pastry. Glass/ceramic inserts—one near the cooktop, one under the warming unit—are landing pads for hot pots and dishes.

The wood-topped island serves as a traffic controller, separating the cooking work area from the dish storage and cleanup center. The island contains the dishwasher and a second sink; both units face away from the cooking center, allowing the dishwasher to be loaded or unloaded without disturbing the cook.

Dish storage is convenient to each eating area. Everyday dishes are stored in open shelves facing the family eating area. China, silver, and serving pieces are in cabinets near the dining room entrance. The china storage area also contains a warming unit for keeping hot foods hot and a buffet serving counter.

A large pantry cabinet is opposite the china storage. Both the cabinet and its doors contain shallow shelves, so all foodstuffs are visible for easy selection.

Architect: Jack A. Woodson.

ANOTHER VIEW (left) shows rest of kitchen, open dish shelves. **Right:** *Cabinets hold china, silver, warming unit.*

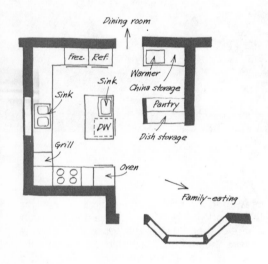

PANTRY STORAGE contains shallow shelves in cabinet doors as well as inside cabinet. All items are visible, handy to reach for easy selection.

APED WORK SPACE *uses island as extra counter.*

MAIN WORK AREA is almost square, providing plenty of counter space and ample storage.

All·white... easy to clean

The owners wanted a modern kitchen large enough for five people to work in, yet they also wanted to retain the atmosphere of their 80-year-old house. The requirements they gave the architect included a cooktop with six burners, two ovens, a separate baking area, and a built-in family eating area.

Instead of the standard wall ovens and separate cooktop, two drop-in stove units were installed. This provided eight burners (two more than they specified) and two self-cleaning ovens that didn't require wall space. The ventilation hood serves both stove units and incorporates lighting.

Blue accents brighten the white kitchen. Since easy cleaning was vital to maintain this kitchen's appearance, all materials selected are easy to clean. Counters are covered with white plastic laminate, and the cabinets with washable paint. Blue ceramic tiles trim the hood, and washable wallpaper echoes the tile pattern.

The family's favorite area is the built-in family eating corner and the soda fountain opposite the table.

Architect: Henry Blackard.

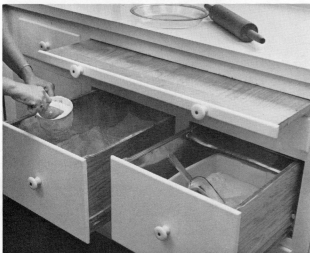

SPECIALIZED STORAGE (top left) over refrigerator has vertical shelves for baking sheets and pans, serving trays, portable cutting board. **Bottom left:** Baking center contains extra-wide pull-out board; metal-lined drawers for flour, sugar.
Above: Lazy-susan corner cabinets utilize hard-to-reach space for canned goods storage.

FAMILY EATING AREA (above) with built-in benches, refrigerator/freezer are outside main work area. China, silver storage cabinets at far left of sink counter. **Left:** Ice cream fountain contains sink, storage for fountain glassware.

Short on space, long on efficiency

When the owner/architect moved from a roomy, Victorian-style home with a large kitchen into the small, hard-working space of a new townhouse, he tried to reproduce all the storage, counter space, and functions the old kitchen offered in the minimal space allotted.

Achieving his goal required compromises. Instead of a kitchen table, a snack counter was installed. Constructed of laminated maple and lowered from the normal counter height, it doubles as a chopping block. The other countertops are plastic laminate edged in maple. Cabinets and wall surfaces are oil-finished, 1-by-4, tongue-and-groove Douglas fir flooring, and the floor is oak hardwood finished with satin polyurethane. All surfaces are easy to clean.

Since there wasn't room for a counter cooktop and wall ovens, he used a combination gas stove with a large oven. Appliances were moved into a wall garage keeping counter space free.

A hinged, bifold door opens to the dining room and closes to conceal kitchen clutter. A sliding window at the snack counter becomes a pass-through for guests on the deck. Both features allow the cook to be close to guests without having them underfoot.

Architect: Thomas Higley.

BOX (left) with handhold serves as chair at snack counter.
Right: *Turned, it becomes a stool to reach overhead storage.*

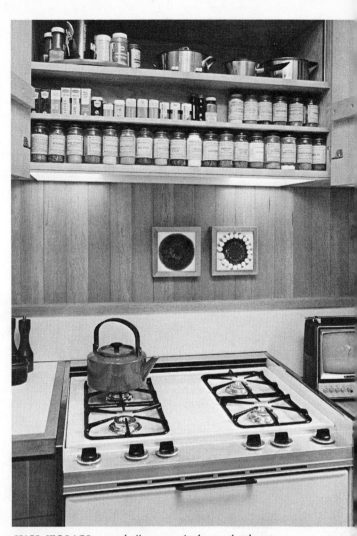

SPICE STORAGE uses shallow area in front of exhaust fan. Dual light fixtures illuminate stove.

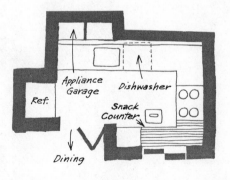

SMALL APPLIANCES are stored in sliding door garage. Power outlet strip is at rear of cabinet.

OMPACT KITCHEN gives 99 square feet of efficiency.

COOKING UTENSILS, pots, and pans hanging from hooks are easy to reach, and add a decorative touch to kitchen.

NARROW OPEN SHELVING displays glasses, cups, other dishes; wooden protective edging holds them in place.

In many older houses, a wall separates the kitchen and breakfast nook. The owner/architect of this kitchen removed the separating wall and, by rearranging cabinets and appliances, brought in more light and provided more storage and open space.

Now that the old wall has gone, a bigger area can take advantage of available light. The skylight over the breakfast table—which once illuminated only the kitchen—now brightens the former nook area, as well. And tearing out the old wall also made room for the addition of another window over the sink counter.

The old cooktop and oven were removed to allow for a new door between the kitchen and bedrooms. A new cooktop was built into the countertop near the sink, and the oven replaced the refrigerator in an alcove. The refrigerator was moved into the kitchen work triangle, adjacent to the counter and sink. In this way, an efficient work area was created with few changes in existing wiring or plumbing.

Since the room is too narrow for ordinary storage cabinets along both long walls, very shallow shelves were installed. They serve as display racks for cups, glasses, and pitchers. Pots and pans hang flat from hooks attached to perforated particle board.

A piece of wood trim forms a lip on the upper shelves to hold glasses and cups in place. On the dish shelf (see photo on opposite page) a 1-inch by 2-inch oak strip was installed, forming an "earthquake bar" to protect the ceramic dishes handcrafted by the owner. Shelves over the counter are open to display the dishes. There are no doors to bump heads on.

Shelves by the stairs hold canned goods.

Architect: Robert Herman.

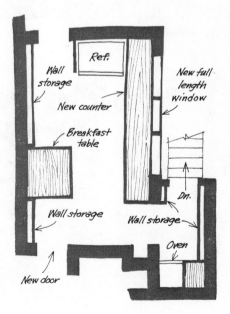

LOFTY CEILING with skylight dominates kitchen.

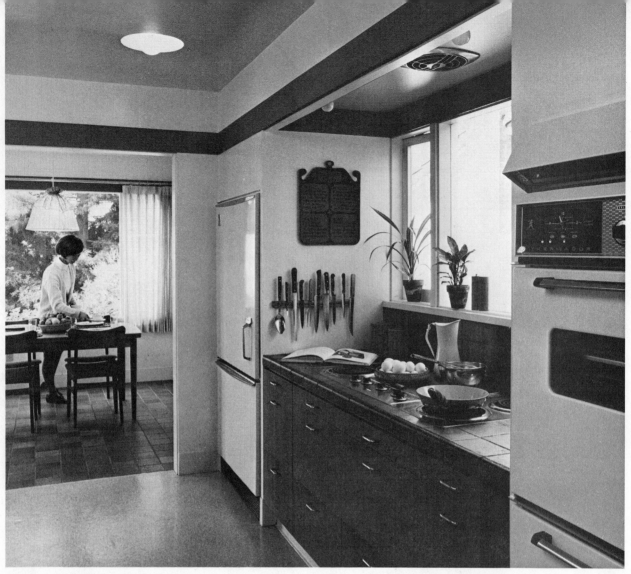

COOKING AREA is large, containing refrigerator, cooktop, wall ovens. Ventilating fan, lighting is concealed by soffit.

Remodeling creates a new wing

This began as a modest deck-and-stairway project to eliminate an inside stairway. As the work progressed, more and more possibilities were seen; the final remodeling produced a new kitchen wing—a well-planned pullman or two-wall kitchen, opening at one end into a breakfast room and at the other, to a much used sewing room-kitchen office. The 5½-foot-wide "corridor" through the kitchen area permits limited foot traffic without inconveniencing the cook.

The architect didn't use the full width of the original room. To lessen the number of steps between the cooktop and the sink, he moved the counter and lower cabinets along the inside wall toward the center of the room. Above this counter, he used the increased space between the new backsplash and the original wall for upper cabinets and two tin-lined storage bins. Since the upper cabinets don't project at all, the counter work space is unhampered.

Architect: Charles D. Stickney.

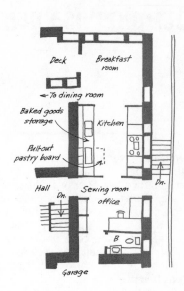

COMBINATION SEWING ROOM/OFFICE was created near kitchen. Low table is right height for sewing, typing; desk used for menu planning.

SINK COUNTER (above) has wooden insert for cutting, chopping. Dishwasher is near sink, breakfast room for easy meal clean-up. **Top left:** Space between backsplash and original wall is used for tin-lined storage bins. **Bottom left:** Laminated wood board for pastry making pulls out below drawers and from behind cabinet doors.

Multi-purpose peninsula

This peninsula is versatile. A cook can work on one side of the 6-foot-wide counter, with plenty of room on the other side for a helper or two. The counter separates kitchen work areas from dining and family activity areas. Double overhead cabinets hold food, cooking utensils, and other cooking aids—pots and pans on the kitchen side, dishes and cook books facing the dining area. Below the book shelves is desk space with a chair and telephone. A long, narrow shelf holds spices at a convenient height.

The rest of the kitchen is close by. The sink and refrigerator are a few steps from the peninsula; ovens are on a side wall.

The 24-inch-square marble counter insert is for candy and pastry making. Cakes are the specialty of the house, and the insert and its surrounding counter are used for cooling the cakes, then frosting and decorating them.

Architect: Lawrence Steiner.

PARQUETED COUNTERTOP is of teak flooring, contains marble insert for making pastries, candy, or icing cakes.

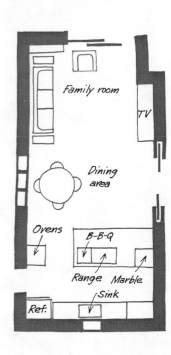

PENINSULA is cooking center, contains cooktop and barbecue grill. Skylight overhead provides natural lighting.

NEAT-AS-A-PIN kitchen is easy to clean, stays uncluttered and presentable between meals.

A no·nonsense kitchen

This kitchen suits the life style of a young and active family with 2 small children. They wanted the kitchen to be the center of things, open to all rooms, yet neat and tidy most of the time.

The husband, an architect, has offices at home, and his clients are apt to walk through at any time. He planned the cabinets to store and organize everything.

The kitchen is positioned so the cook can keep an eye on the children in the living room and look beyond to a pool outside. The plastic laminate cabinet fronts and counters are scrubbable. To the left of the sink, a nonscratch ceramic chopping block can double as a food warmer for short periods of time.

When the family entertains guests, any kitchen clutter can be hidden behind louvered shutters, but the kitchen is usually open, immaculate and ready to use.

For another view of this kitchen see the cover photograph.

Architect: James Flynn.

SMALL APPLIANCE GARAGE shares large storage area, has electric outlet so appliances are ready to use.

COZY KITCHEN is reminiscent of a Western movie set with old cooking stove, wood burner, rustic materials.

Handcrafted for the rustic look

SWINGING DOORS are distinctive, decorated with whimsical cutouts and branches from trees instead of slats.

HANGING PLANTS surround skylight; kitchen table is below.

Twigs for drawer pulls? A shingled interior wall? A hanging garden in the kitchen? Why not? All these and other unusual features fit beautifully into this remodeled cabin in the woods.

Modern efficiency was not the prime concern during this kitchen's conception, but it works well for the owners. In the farmhouse tradition, the cozy room serves as the family's gathering spot.

The owners' collection of antiques and antiquated objects perform many tasks: an old wood-burning iron stove provides heat; an early 1900s gas stove does the cooking and baking; old fruit jars store herbs, spices, and beans; weathered boards and shingles cover the walls and conceal the refrigerator; used brick forms a fire wall for the wood burner.

The skylight and sloping ceiling provide modern touches. Natural lighting serves people and plants.

The work triangle is large, so the patchwork-covered table can double as an island during meal preparation.

Design: S. E. Marugg, Beryl Hooper.

TILED SINK COUNTER also serves stove. Cabinets of weathered wood have twisted branches for drawer pulls.

PREPARATION AREA (left) has laminated wood insert for chopping, cutting tasks. Floor is quarry tile. **Above:** *Modern refrigerator hides behind wooden door to retain kitchen's rustic atmosphere.*

MOBILE TABLE with hardwood top rolls wherever extra work space is needed. Surface is good for cutting, chopping.

His and hers kitchen

MARBLE-TOPPED PENINSULA is main work area, family eating counter. Surface good for making pastry, candy.

FOOD PREPARATION and cleanup centers around main triple-bowl sink and dishwasher. Spice shelf is handy to preparation center, cooktop.

When the owners purchased this house, the kitchen was the first room to be remodeled. It was planned down to the smallest detail; then the ideas were taken to the designer, who checked them, drew up blueprints, and supervised the construction.

Because the man of the house likes to prepare specialty dishes, the kitchen was planned to accommodate two cooks. Since the owners sometimes entertain large groups of people, room was allocated for the equivalent of a butler's pantry between the kitchen proper and the dining room.

This service cleanup area is almost a second kitchen. It has a refrigerator (also used by the children for soft drinks), sink, dishwasher, outlets for appliances, and a warming center (see photo at right).

Design: Fred Blair Green.

SERVING COUNTER is close to dining room, away from work areas. It contains two built-in warming drawers and a food warmer located in cabinet over counter for dishes, foods.

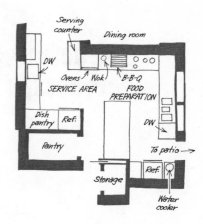

MAJOR CLEANUP AREA contains second sink, dishwasher, china and silver storage; serving counter is opposite.

L-SHAPED WORK AREA contains dishwasher, sink, cooktop, wall ovens. Small appliances fit under counter shelf.

Redefining space creates efficiency

By redefining an over-sized one-wall kitchen, the owners gained more efficient kitchen work space and an informal eating area. The work triangle is tighter, appliances and kitchen storage are more accessible, and the raised counter designating the two areas also blocks any kitchen clutter from the view of diners.

The raised dividing counter also serves as a small appliance garage. Strip electrical outlets keep appliances ready to use, and their recessed storage frees counter space.

The chopping block counter is lowered to a better working height for cutting and stirring; the knife insert keeps knives and sharpener close at hand. A roll-around stool is stored underneath the counter.

Windows and sliding glass doors in the eating area bring the outdoors in and provide natural light.

In the eating area, built-in dish storage frees kitchen cabinets for foodstuffs and cooking utensils.

Design: Jean Kirsch.

PANTRY CABINET (far left) utilizes area between refrigerator, door. **Left:** Cabinet moves on drawer slides, casters.

SPICES, HERBS are kept in drawers below chopping board.

STORAGE FOR LINENS (left), glassware, dishes opens to family eating area. Open shelves on wall with cabinets below complete dish storage. **Above:** Ventilating hood contains warming units; fold-down racks hold casseroles, plates.

Parts of this kitchen sailed the high seas

The idea for this kitchen was spawned several years ago when the owners visited a salvage shop for ship parts. They spotted a heavily painted, 9-foot cabinet— its doors askew, its hinges blackened—and bought it. While refinishing, they were delighted to discover beautifully grained oak and solid brass fittings—made to a ship's high standards of craftsmanship.

One nautical piece led to another, and eventually they had enough to outfit a kitchen. With the help of an architect, they installed the cabinets, occasionally adding small sections of new oak to complete the sea-to-land transition. Floors are oak, countertops a slate-like plastic laminate. The resulting kitchen makes galley work more enjoyable, with no pitch and roll!

If you'd like to find some nautical pieces, it's still possible; shipwreckers in some of the coastal cities have salvaged brass and cabinetwork. Look under Scrap Metals in the yellow pages of the telephone book. Ask for firms that handle ships' salvage or inquire at marine supply stores. Prices are reasonable if you consider the quality of the wood and fittings. You'll have a distinctive piece when you're through, but count on a lot of rubbing in between.

Architect: Walter Hansen.

OAK WALL CABINET (left) once held medical supplies on a yacht. **Above:** Wooden dish rack held dishes secure during ship's roll. Dishes lift up and out for daily use.

BRASS DOORKNOB (above) is typical of hardware used on ships. **Right:** Bookracks once used by a ship's navigator now hold cook books, television set, towels.

NAUTICAL KITCHEN from ship-worn parts: cabinets from cargo ship; brass stools from ferryboat.

LONG COUNTER contains entire kitchen including wall ovens, cooktop, sink, dishwasher, refrigerator/freezer.

A one·wall kitchen that works

With 14 feet of hardwood counter between the wall ovens and the refrigerator, this remodeled kitchen doesn't conform to the compact working triangle usually considered ideal. Yet the owner found that it works beautifully.

Before the remodeling, the kitchen was 12 feet square and shared the remainder of its present space with a screened porch. Eliminating the porch, along with some doors that routed too much traffic through the kitchen, created one large room with windows on three sides. Two of these windows function as pass-throughs to a new deck.

The table in the center of the room provides a central working space that would otherwise be missing. Besides serving as a barrier to keep spectators out of the cook's way, it serves all the needs of kitchen counter space—it's a resting spot for groceries on their way to the food pantry, a work table for both the cook and her children, a family dining table, and on occasion a place for informal dinners.

Open shelves over the counter store everyday dishes, frequently used casseroles, and cooking utensils. Recessed soffit lighting illuminates working surfaces.

Architects: Beebe-Hersey.

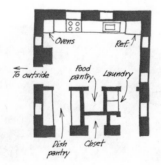

Peninsula is major work area

This peninsula divider provides for a wide variety of kitchen activities. One side has a cooktop, chopping block, and spice storage. On the other side, an eating counter seats four; it houses storage drawers just underneath and a phone jack at the end.

The divider stands 30 inches high—the standard height for a kitchen table but 6 inches lower than standard for a cooktop. However, the owner finds the reduced height easier for stirring pots on the range and more convenient for using the chopping block. Self-ventilating cooktop doesn't require an overhead fan.

A narrow counter—flush with wall counters—protects the eating area from steam and spattering grease. At mealtime, it's a handy place to put serving dishes.

Chairs of standard height fit at the eating counter. Between meals, this area becomes a quiet nook for planning menus, making telephone calls, or watching television.

Architect: Derk Vyn.

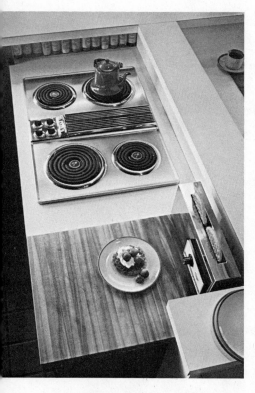

COOKING SIDE (above) of peninsula has self-ventilating four-burner cooktop, chopping block, spices stored under counter. **Right:** Narrow raised counter divides two areas.

An interior room flooded with light

BIRD'S EYE VIEW (below) from hallway overhead shows entire kitchen. Clockwise from top: refrigerator/freezer, pantry, snack counter, sink, stove. **Right:** Pass-through opens to low buffet counter in dining room.

PASS-THROUGH (above) opening to gallery, living room is handy for serving snacks. **Right:** Skylight brings natural light into kitchen, upper hall. High ceiling gives a spacious feeling to the room.

If you were to drop a kitchen into the center of a house, you'd expect it to be dark and dreary. That's why this bright kitchen is a surprise.

The huge skylight illuminates the two-story kitchen and the second-floor hall. Natural light makes the kitchen bright and pleasant during the daytime; area and spotlights take over at night to flood working centers with plenty of light. The over-counter cabinets are recessed to provide more usable counter area and to eliminate shadows from working centers.

Every side of the kitchen opens to an adjacent room, making the kitchen function as the hub of the house and eliminating a closed-in feeling. Pass-throughs to gallery and dining areas make food and refreshments more accessible for serving and entertaining. Casual family meals are served in an eating area beyond the small snack island.

Architects: Matlin & Dvoretzky.

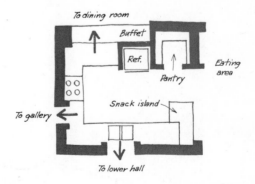

COOK HAS full view of kitchen, office, eating area. Eating counter is lowered to table height.

An L
within a larger L

This kitchen keeps the cook in the midst of family activities but out of the traffic. The owner/architect used an L-shaped island inside an L-shaped kitchen to create meal preparation, eating, office, and family activity areas that are in a single room yet don't interfere with each other.

So the room won't look too much like a kitchen, most storage is below the island counter. Carefully arranged bins, shelves, and drawers hold all the pots, pans, cooking utensils, canned goods, and spices. Each cabinet is constructed as a single unit with shelves attached to the cabinet front. The entire unit slides forward on metal drawer slides so every inch of storage space is easily reached. The eating area, slightly lower in height than the cooktop, completes the L separating kitchen and living areas.

The home office takes up one wall next to the eating island. Attached to the overhead cabinets are book shelves and open bins for records and correspondence. Large filing drawers are located under the counter. Windows between the counter and overhead storage run the length of the office counter; they let in light and fresh air.

The activity area is used for family gatherings and informal entertaining.

Architect: Robert W. Champion.

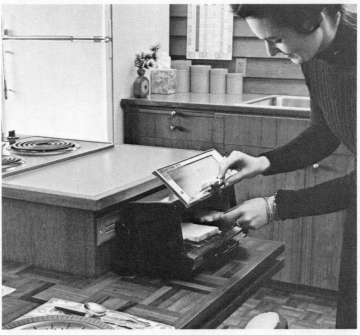

SPICE CABINET has shallow storage for easy selection. Pull-out boards increase counter space.

TOASTER has niche with electrical outlet under cooktop, is handy to diners seated at parqueted eating counter, same parquet as floor.

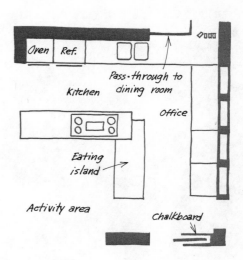

CHALKBOARD at end of office area is sheet of plastic laminate matching kitchen countertops. It's handy for writing family reminders, grocery lists.

If a well-ordered work area brings out the experimental cook in you, here's a kitchen plan to consider. Every aspect is coordinated to make cooking tasks easy to perform.

The main U-shaped work center is well equipped; it incorporates a refrigerator/freezer, a combination wooden chopping block/pass-through counter, small appliance center, dishwasher, sink, cooktop, barbecue grill, warming drawer, and wall ovens. The wood-topped island provides additional work space as well as controlling traffic. If a large gathering calls for extra kitchen helpers, the island is built on casters and can be wheeled away to free floor space.

The ventilating hood was installed at a higher-than-normal height to allow the cook adequate head room while working at the cooktop or grill. The owners found grilling oily foods created excess smoke, so they designed a metal screen to trap the accumulation. When the grill is in use, a piece of sheet metal swings down to hide the smoke; when idle, the screen attaches to the inner hood with heavy-duty magnets.

The opposite wall (see photo next page) contains two tiled counters, a planning desk, and lots of storage area. The counters double as buffet serving areas for large, informal groups. The desk has space for cook books, a telephone, and a writing surface for menu planning and correspondence.

The kitchen is accessible to the dining room, family eating area, and patio, making it the hub of family activities.

PASS-THROUGH COUNTER (left) doubles as baking center; mixer is stored in appliance garage at right. **Right:** Planning center is well-equipped, has built-in desk, telephone, shelves for cook books.

VENTILATING HOOD (left) serves both cooktop and barbecue grill. Colorful, patterned ceramic tile is used for backsplash. **Right:** When barbecue grill is in use, metal screen swings down to trap excess smoke; when not needed, screen attaches to inner hood with industrial magnets.

HAPED KITCHEN as viewed from pass-through.

VIEW FROM SINK shows new work area, back counter. Perforated hardboard is used as backsplash throughout.

U•shaped kitchen filled with ideas

When the owner/architect purchased a small, older house, remodeling the kitchen was the first project.

Traffic presented a serious problem in the original plan. Because it had to go somewhere, he moved the entrance to the dining room to a position opposite a doorway leading into a hallway. This shifted traffic to one end of the kitchen.

Since this pathway separated that end from the rest of the kitchen, he decided to emphasize its separateness. The counter was dropped to a mixing height of 32 inches and was covered with white plastic laminate instead of the pumpkin-colored plastic used in the rest of the kitchen. When the owners entertain the counter serves as a buffet, with guests entering from the hallway or the dining room and circulating past it.

With its generous storage cabinets, this area also functions as a pantry and baking center. It even contains an extra-wide pull-out board that can serve as an eating counter.

For easy service to the dining room, a narrow pass-through was opened at kitchen counter level. Below it, storage space opens to the dining room for china, serving pieces.

Architect: Daniel H. Goltz.

PASS-THROUGH to dining room can be opened or closed by shutters. Dining room storage is underneath.

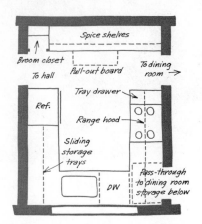

PULL-OUT CUTTING BOARD (left) in back counter is extra-wide, serves as eating counter, kitchen desk. Perforated hardboard provides additional utensil storage. **Above:** *Narrow space beside stove unit is used as storage for serving trays, baking sheets, muffin pans.*

MAPLE COUNTER is perfect for making pastry, cutting and chopping tasks. Cooking utensils hang from hooks.

The country kitchen... updated

This cook believes that a kitchen should be big enough for family and friends. The remodeling pictured here gave the cook the well organized space needed.

The original 65-year-old kitchen was quite generous (10 by 18½ feet) but not really large enough for good organization of the various work areas, so the north wall was pushed out 4½ feet to incorporate what had been a back porch. A large window and skylight were added to the extension to bring in daylight. The extension contains the sink and adjacent counter space, as well as a maple-surfaced counter for chopping and pastry making.

One wall holds the stove and refrigerator with a counter between. The opposite wall has a bar sink, storage, and a small deck. A dining table occupies the central space.

Architects: Joyce, Copeland, Vaughan.

SKYLIGHT (left) in new kitchen extension provides daylight, open feeling in major work area. Extension also created counter space, storage. **Above left:** *Desk area is for menu planning, correspondence. Counter with bar sink, wine storage doubles as beverage bar.* **Above right:** *Tiled counter takes hot pots, ovenware from adjacent stove.*

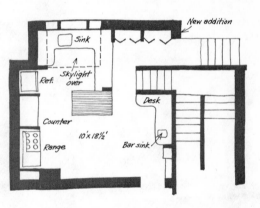

VENERABLE GAS STOVE has its own corner. Spices, utensils are ready to use.

Room to throw parties in

This kitchen is what happened when a home owner with a wild enthusiasm for wood decided to remodel a 40-year-old kitchen. He engaged an architect to do the designing, then he executed the plans on weekends. A gifted woodworker, he slowly built each cabinet in his workshop and stored them in the garage until all were finished.

The result is a generous, comfortable room, large enough for a group of people to move around in easily. The cantilevered table is used as a work surface, for family eating, and for informal entertaining. The built-in music center (see photo next page) adds a special dimension.

This U-shaped kitchen creates a natural work flow pattern: food progresses from the wood-covered refrigerator to the chopping block, sink, cooktop, and finally to the table at the end. The opposite side of the room is used mainly when the family is entertaining, but doubles as a baking center.

Architect: Mark Mills.

STEREO SYSTEM (left) is built into kitchen, perfect for a cook who spends a lot of time in the kitchen. Speakers are above and to either side of refrigerator. **Center:** Stained glass windows were designed by owners, made by a professional in colors of amber, gold, touches of orange. **Right:** Entertainment counter has bar sink, long tiled area for buffet serving.

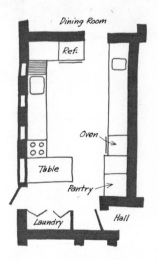

CANTILEVERED TABLE is same height as counters, giving extra work space. Laundry area is behind bifold doors, handy to table for folding clothes.

N KITCHEN is perfect for informal parties.

KITCHEN WORK AREA uses one-wall plan, see diagram page 6. Counter has no overhead storage.

Four·function island controls kitchen

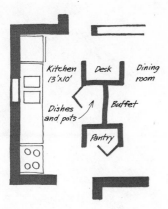

Kitchen 13'x10'   Desk   Dining room

Dishes and pots   Buffet

Pantry

Every inch of space in this kitchen measures up to two requirements—ease of cooking and economy of construction.

The architect designed a four-function island, which gives easy-to-see storage and acts as a divider (no wall needed) between the kitchen and dining room. Costly cabinetwork is limited, and everything the cook needs is stocked within close reach.

Each side of the island is a compact unit. The kitchen side takes the place of conventional hanging wall cabinets; it houses dishes and utensils in floor-to-ceiling shelves. A built-in buffet serving area faces the dining room, with storage for dishes, linens, and wine. The other two sides of the island serve as pantry storage and kitchen office with space for files and cook books.

Architect: Walter Hansen.

DISHES, cooking utensils are stored in kitchen side of island. Shelves are adjustable for efficient storage.

BUFFET SERVING AREA (left) on dining room side of island. **Above:** *Office planning center at one end of island.*

Roomy enough for two good cooks

COUNTER (below) is major work center, contains dishwasher, sink, cutting board, cooktop, ovens.
Right: *Shallow spice storage is handy to cooktop.*

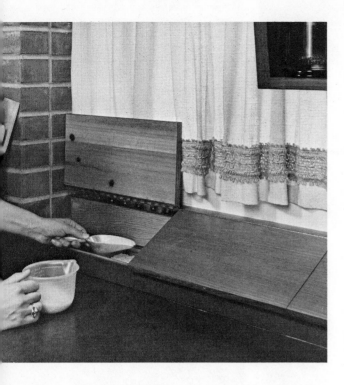

STORAGE BINS (above) line long counter, hold flour, sugar, rice, pastas, other staples in stainless steel canisters. **Right:** *Counter beside refrigerator is small appliance work area. Wall cabinet shares pass-through dish storage with dining room.*

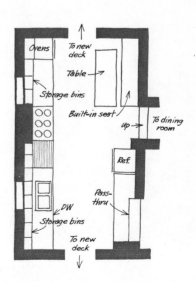

The owners of this kitchen, part-owners of a restaurant and excellent cooks themselves, chose the one-wall plan as best suited to their style of cooking and entertaining. They found the necessary space by converting an unused garage.

With 6 feet of floor space between the main work counter and the opposite counter, they have plenty of room to work around each other. Since the owners enjoy entertaining with small formal dinners, both can be in the kitchen at the last minute. The table and built-in bench allow guests to watch the action. And for the single cook, the standard work triangle between sink, cooktop, and refrigerator is still compact.

The real hub of the kitchen is around the cooktop and the adjacent built-in cutting board. Tools and utensils are stored where they are most used; the equipment is of professional quality.

Countertops are of black matte-finished seamless asbestos, with a factory-applied vinyl coating. The cabinets are constructed of teak.

Both ends of the kitchen open onto decks.

Architect: Hal Gilbert.

U-SHAPED KITCHEN (left) was created from recycled materials. **Right:** *Bottom-hinged door conceals garbage can.*

Recycled kitchen for the ecology·minded

Everything in this kitchen has a new lease on life, depending on how the owner, a graphic artist and furniture builder, found use for it.

The redwood came from a wine fermenting tank 16 feet tall, but each piece, 3 inches thick, has been re-milled into three pieces of varying thickness and rough finish. Wall studs are old 2 by 4s. Shelves arrived from the old porch steps of an old house. On the counter are ceramic tile seconds with used oak-floor edging strips. Decorative tiles above the sink were salvaged from an old tile factory. Pots, pans, and tools hang from a railroad tie, each hook a different vintage and each with a history.

Plumbing fascinates the owner. During this remodel he found a pipe going from floor to ceiling in the tool rack area. He decided he liked it and let it remain. He made the movable recipe stand from Victorian banister turnings, using halves of copper toilet bowl floats for candle holders.

Both of the owners have their own cooking specialties. The kitchen is wide enough for both to cook at once and even has two chopping boards.

Design: Al Garvey.

Kitchen with a Mexican flavor

Although well supplied with all the modern conveniences, this room has the feeling of an old Mexican or southwestern ranch-style kitchen. The major walls, like those in the rest of the house, are adobe. A large metal hood extends over the cooktop and barbecue grill, and skillets hang from a wrought-iron rack.

Colorful Mexican tile covers the wall behind the stove; one row continues around the countertops as a decorative and protective backsplash. The drawers and cabinets are stained a dark walnut. The concrete floor is light brown, scored to resemble tile.

Several people can work together here without getting in each other's way. The L-shaped plan provides a total of about 32 feet of work counter, with sinks and the cooktop sensibly spaced along it.

Architect: James T. Flynn.

PLACEMATS, linens are kept in shallow, pull-out shelves.

LARGE METAL HOOD serves cooktop, barbecue grill. Colorful Mexican tiles form backsplash, decorative trim. Wrought-iron pan rack adds to Mexican feeling.

New... but the old charm remains

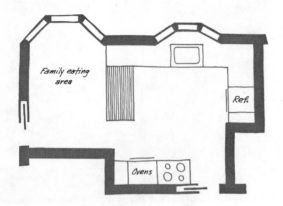

Many people who buy older houses to renovate find the kitchens awkward to work in and badly in need of updating. The owners of this kitchen wanted a modern, efficient room that would still retain the charm of their vintage house.

During the remodeling, they discovered a brick chimney wall and decided to leave it exposed. They installed wooden cabinets, created bay windows—one behind the sink and one in the family eating area—and selected patterned, multi-colored tile for the counter backsplash. The background color of the tiles is repeated in the tiled countertop. Gingham-patterned wallpaper adds to the country kitchen atmosphere.

The modernized U-shaped work area provides plenty of work space—enough for two or three cooks to work at the same time. The wooden chopping block peninsula is perfect for cutting and chopping tasks and for pastry making. It also serves as a snack counter, permitting family and friends to chat with the cook without being underfoot.

The cooktop and wall ovens are located opposite the sink. Ample pot and pan storage is provided in drawers beneath the cooktop, while a large pantry cabinet holds food items. Over the cooktop, the custom-built ventilating hood contains a copper insert which adds a cheery glow to the kitchen.

COOKING CENTER (left) contains cooktop, wall ovens. **Below:** *Large drawers hold pots, pans, ovenware. Cupboard door has shallow shelves for spices, herbs.*

SWITCHES, electrical outlets, lighting units hide under overhead cabinets to avoid marring tiles.

Cook enjoys a garden view

Wouldn't this U-shaped kitchen be a delight to cook in? A pleasant garden, the warm feeling of wood-grained walls and floors, and an upholstered bench for back-seat chefs blend with the carefully planned efficiency of the kitchen work arena.

Most food preparation revolves around the special-use centers this kitchen incorporates. Each center stores all necessary equipment and supplies for its specialized tasks. These centers include an office for planning, a baking center, a bricked indoor barbecue, and a family eating area surrounded by the garden.

Even though one completely windowed wall eliminates some overhead storage, the owner found enough space for 20 years' accumulation of equipment. The eating area is shielded from normal cooking disarray by a raised storage counter that doubles as a sink backsplash. A built-in warming tray on the tiled counter is accessible to both kitchen and eating nook.

A wooden cart is in constant use, serving as a small mobile island whenever needed. When not in use, the cart is garaged under the baking center counter (see photo next page).

Design: Janean.

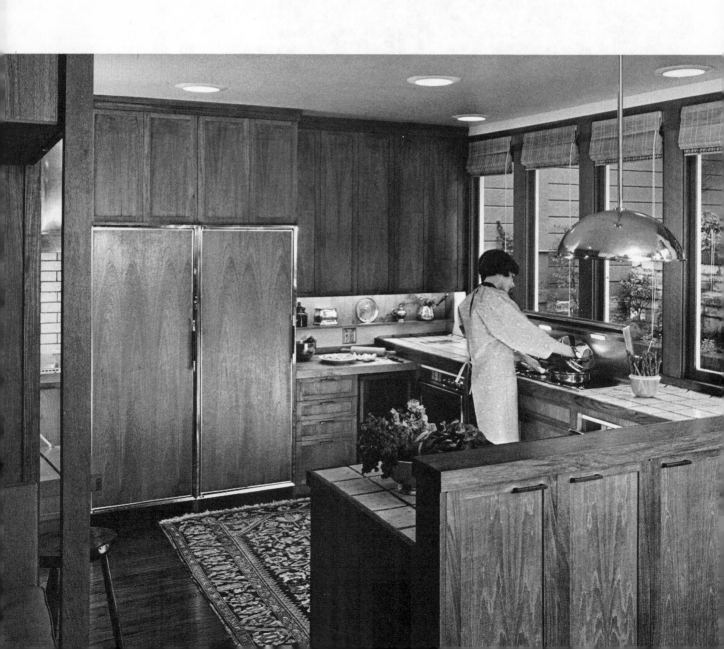

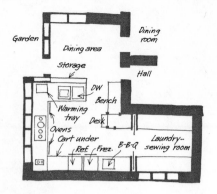

GARDEN VIEW pleases both cook and
diners. Sink counter backsplash
hides kitchen clutter from dining area;
sliding doors conceal storage.

BAKING CENTER has lowered wooden working surface for
making pastry. Metal-lined drawers hold flour, sugar.

DESK AREA contains cook books, telephone, writing surface
for meal planning. Bench has extra storage below.

BARBECUE CENTER permits year-around grilling. Surrounding surfaces are tiled for easy maintenance.

SHAPED kitchen is open, airy, easy to work in.

MAIN WORK AREA uses two-wall plan: cooktop and sink on one side, refrigerator/freezer and wall ovens opposite.

T·formation floor plan controls traffic

Keeping the cook's work area free from unnecessary traffic was the primary concern of this owner/architect. The first remodeling step was to make the two-wall kitchen a dead end—a corridor leading nowhere. Its size, 8 by 12 feet, discourages loitering.

Next, the dish storage and cleanup areas were taken from the cooking center and located at the top end of the "T", with a pathway between. The children can set or clear the tables and load the dishwasher without bothering the cook. A second sink eliminates "I want a drink of water" intruders.

This functional kitchen is easy to maintain. Counters are laminated wood. Tile inserts on either side of the cooktop receive hot pots or pans from the cooktop or ovens. A recessed cupboard above the sink increases headroom; spices and herbs are stored here, one row deep for easy selection. A menu planning center is located beside the refrigerator.

Since wall space is minimal, windows crop up in unexpected places. Small panes are tucked under overhead cabinets. The dead-end wall contains a large window which frames a tree. A large skylight in the peaked ceiling lets in sunlight; an indoor shutter conceals it on hot days.

Architect: George Cody.

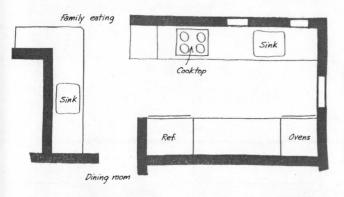

CLEANUP AREA (left) has sink, dishwasher out of cook's way. **Right:** Menu planning area stores cook books.

COVERED SKYLIGHT (far left) keeps out unwanted sunlight, heat. **Left:** Shutter is set on tracks, is opened or closed with extension pole.

U-SHAPED WORK CENTER contains six-burner cooktop, grill, deep sink with gooseneck faucet for filling large pots.

Everything's in view in this kitchen

WOOD-TOPPED CART rolls where needed. When not in use, cart tucks under counter between ovens and refrigerator.

SWEDISH STORAGE UNIT is built into backsplash, contains flour, sugar, peas, pasta, other condiments.

EATING NOOK adjoins kitchen. Corner cabinets store serving pieces, books, decorative objects. Door at left leads to dining room.

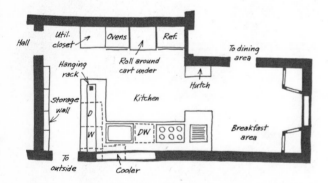

The owner of this kitchen wanted everything in full view. No more searching and rummaging for her!

The designer created this kitchen and breakfast area by combining a service porch, kitchen, and breakfast room into one large room. The owner wanted to be able to cut on any surface, so all countertops were constructed of laminated maple. She wanted to see all her storage, so conventional overhead cabinets were replaced by open shelves, racks, and cabinets with wire mesh fronts for selection at-a-glance. A six-burner cooktop and a grill handle her cooking requirements.

A roll-around island with a maple top for chopping gets constant use throughout the kitchen. When not needed, the cart is stationed under a counter between the refrigerator and the wall ovens.

Design: Ray Kennedy.

WIRE MESH covers storage cabinet doors; all pantry items are visible for easy selection.

Kitchen for a crowd

Like a small efficient restaurant, this kitchen has the equipment and counters needed to feed eight children and still allow for the smooth flow of food preparation, serving, and cleanup.

The architect's problem was to design a kitchen with enough room for 10 people to maneuver and work. The owners' requirements included ample counter space, a distinct baking area, built-in chopping boards in several places, and easy-to-maintain counters and floors. The original kitchen wall was pushed out 17 feet to gain needed space and window light. The new, soaring ceiling contributes to the spacious feeling.

The island allows several people to work at once on different sides and provides extra counter space and storage. Another counter at the opening of the U (see floor plan next page) helps direct traffic away from kitchen activities; it also doubles as a buffet counter and snack center.

Because of sheer numbers, many facilities needed to be doubled. This kitchen contains two sinks, two warming ovens, two baking ovens, two refrigerators, two cooktops, and plenty of working space on both ceramic and wood countertops. There's enough room and equipment for family participation.

Architect: George Cody.

TILED COUNTER (left) between kitchen, family room has dishwasher, second sink. **Above left:** *Baking center contains built-in sifters for flour, sugar. Units slide out for refilling.* **Above right:** *Metal-lined drawers store rice and noodles. Plastic, perforated, pull-out bins hold potatoes, oranges, other fresh produce.*

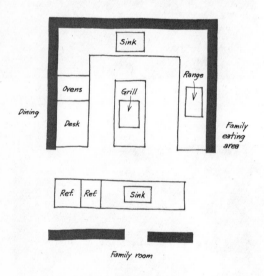

WRAP-AROUND WINDOWS provide light, view for cook. Chopping block beside sink aids in rinsing, chopping chores.

ACIOUS KITCHEN has room for many cook's helpers.

ANTIQUE STOVE (left) dominates kitchen. **Right:** *Fireman's pole gives children quick access to family eating area.*

Turn of the century revisited

The owners bought a 1916 stove with two ovens and six burners and, coincidentally, purchased a house built the same year. They asked the architect to design a country kitchen around it and other antiques they'd acquired. Three rooms were combined into one, including a cooking area, dining table, and play space.

A place to enjoy family and friends, the kitchen is the center of their household. The three boys are vigorous and never seem to slow down. Sometimes they join in kitchen activities helping to bake a cake or make marmalade.

The owner is a mood cook; she approaches meals with a flexible attitude, using whatever supplies are around. A soup pot is usually going on the stove, giving the kitchen a lived-in atmosphere.

Architect: William Logan.

POTS, PANS hang from hooks on bicycle-wheel rack. Wheel spins with touch of finger to reach pot you want.

Low cooking island for a petite cook

A petite cook who needed low counter working space presented a design problem for her architects. The solution: a low central island where she can work with ease, and standard-height counters for the rest of the family.

The island is a large (4 by 9½-foot) preparation center with appliance shelves, knife storage, garbage niche, and a small desk at one end for meal planning. Behind the island, a pass-through to the dining area is the same height as the island and can be closed by folding doors.

Architects: Paul McKim and Associates.

CENTER ISLAND (right) has marble insert for pastry making. Tiled surface is easy to clean. **Above:** Buffet serving counter has pass-through from kitchen, built-in warmer.

WITH DOORS OPEN, cook has view of dining area. Pass-through opens to buffet serving counter.

It's an open and shut kitchen

FOLDING DOORS on piano hinges close to completely hide kitchen clutter, are painted to match paneled walls.

PATTERNED CERAMIC TILES beside cooktop create a heatproof landing pad for hot pots and pans.

BAKING CENTER lowered to 32-inch working height, other counters are 36 inches. Open shelf holds herbs, spices.

The cook who uses this small kitchen considers its size an advantage. Everything is in easy reach; the walking space is 9 feet by 6 feet. Cook and one helper can work without colliding.

A spacious 18-foot-square family room that brings conversation to the cook is adjacent to the kitchen. The family room doubles as an informal dining room for family and for guests. On such occasions the kitchen literally disappears (see photo previous page). But usually it doesn't; it stays unbuttoned, partially on view.

This is a kitchen designed for serious cooking. Its owner has time and likes to use it. Her counters are maple; the sink and drain area are stainless steel, as are cooktop, ovens, and built-in refrigerator. Vegetable cutting, meat trimming, and pastry making take place right on the counters.

Buffet service works well with this layout. The shuttered pass-through, normally open, allows hot dishes to go straight from oven or cooktop to counter.

Design: Janean.

*WOOD-TOPPED COUNTERS (above) can withstand chopping tasks. Knives adhere to magnetic strip. **Left:** Cooking area is convenient to work in. Cooktop has stainless backsplash, easy to clean.*

Designed to display a junk collection

Some stiff requirements guided the architect in this kitchen remodel. The owners wanted an efficient kitchen where the family could gather for meals or a chat and one that would have a distinct, personal quality. As collectors, the owners had pieces they wanted to include—a leaded, stained glass window; a set of post-office boxes with 60 individual units; and old bottle racks.

Since the owners didn't want to add on to the kitchen, the first step was to make the circulation pattern more efficient. The door to the garage was moved to a corner, so the pathway no longer cut the room in half. Simply relocating a door can often solve space problems.

The kitchen's size, 11 by 12 feet, remained the same and plumbing was moved very little. The only structural changes involved adding the stained glass window, the new door to the garage, and the skylight. By tearing out the old kitchen and doing the painting themselves, the owners helped keep costs down.

The cabinets and floor are oak. The counters are laminated maple. A row of ceramic tiles behind the sink serves as a decorative backsplash. A 2-inch by 6-inch maple board is a plant perch.

Architect: Michael Moyer.

OLD BEVERAGE CRATES (above) make handy containers for herbs, spices. Labels attached to bottletops allow easy selection. **Right:** Post-office boxes become a catchall drawer, holding scissors, tape, etc. A sliding button latch replaced original combination locks for quick access.

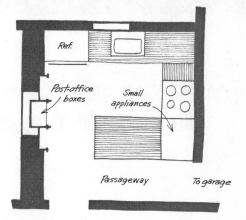

APPLIANCE GARAGE at end of laminated eating counter has electrical outlets inside cabinet to keep wires hidden, appliances ready to use. Appliances are placed on platforms that roll out on counter when needed.

V KITCHEN uses U-shaped work area, storage wall.

NEW KITCHEN is U-shaped with maple counters, marble insert for making pastry. High counter hides old stove.

One kitchen wasn't enough so they added another

This kitchen is really two. They work particularly well for a cook who specializes in exotic foods. Several kinds of dishes can be prepared for a dinner party without running out of room.

When the owners purchased this house, they knew the original kitchen wouldn't be adequate. So with the aid of an architect, the existing breakfast area was remodeled into a second cooking center.

The design for the new kitchen required hiding a favorite old stove, and at the same time providing maximum counter and storage space. A new bar counter doubles as a serving counter for buffet-style dinners.

The new kitchen area contains a second sink, wooden counters for cutting and chopping, and a marble insert for pastry making. The counter has no backsplash, so windows begin counter-high, giving the new area an open airy feeling.

Architect: Donald James Clark.

DISH STORAGE (left) occupies floor-to-ceiling cabinets located on storage wall. Shelves are adjustable for maximum use of space. **Above:** Baking equipment is stored in turntable shelves in a corner of new kitchen. Revolving shelves utilize all space, spin wanted items into view.

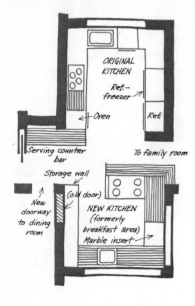

ORIGINAL KITCHEN contains cooktop, wall oven, large refrigerator unit. Hardware, cabinet moldings unify two kitchens.

Table and island can be joined

This compact kitchen work space combines a permanent six-burner cooking island with a movable dining table. When the table is flush with the island, it becomes additional space for food preparation. When the two units are apart, up to 10 people can be seated at the table. This setup is great for the cook, who can keep an eye on the kitchen as well as join in the table conversation.

Both table top and cooking island are constructed of laminated maple. The cooking island was lowered to meet the standard table height. Although this is lower than normal for counter work space, the height is a good one for stirring at the cooktop and chopping or pastry making on the table top.

Architect: Dartmond Cherk.

PUSHED TOGETHER, table is flush with cooktop, adding extra work surface. Cooktop unit is 2 by 6 feet, table 4 by 6 feet.

*PULLED APART (left), work space becomes two separate units, a cooktop area and a family eating table that seats up to 10 people. **Above:** Cooktop island has 2 by 4's that extend 7 inches and slide under table to stabilize the two when joined.*

LONG OAK COUNTER with knife insert is main work surface for preparing fresh vegetables and other foods.

Farm kitchen for a naturalist cook

When the owners purchased an old farmhouse on a long strip of land, they decided to partially remodel the kitchen. Some of the old cabinets were retained, but the new oak countertop and resawn cedar cabinets below it were added. Like most farm kitchens, the room is spacious with a great deal of storage area. It's a kitchen well suited to people who like to grow their own food.

The owners live in a mild climate where they can grow most fruits and vegetables all year around, and they do. The kitchen is located close to the garden, so they can pick, chop, and steam a vegetable within minutes. They didn't include a garbage disposal since they make their own compost. Cooking and gardening are time consuming, but the owners feel the end result is worth it.

Their collection of antique kitchen tools serve as kitchen decorations as well as cooking implements. Design: Bernie Safire.

ANTIQUE KITCHEN TOOLS hang from hooks above counter. Most of these utensils are useful as well as decorative.

U-SHAPED COUNTER with sink, dishwasher, is major work area. Shutters cover unmatched windows for uniform look.

Still spacious but more workable

Fresh paint and new countertops may appear to modernize a kitchen, but they won't solve the real problems if the layout is wrong.

Before remodeling, this kitchen had a 20-foot counter opposite the stove and refrigerator; its large work triangle was awkward and fatiguing for the cook. The architect's solution was to create a smaller, more workable kitchen without losing the feeling of space found in so many Victorian houses.

He moved the sink to a more convenient position, centered opposite the refrigerator and cooktop. This formed a tighter work triangle. The new U-shaped, tiled counter provides more work surface and additional storage within the central work area. By dividing the kitchen into specialized areas, the owners gained an eating counter for the family, a buffet/storage area leading into the dining room, and a wet bar.

Architect: Thomas Higley.

BEVERAGE BAR contains sink, storage for glassware and wine. The buffet serving counter is opposite.

COMPACT COOKING AREA has herbs, spices close at hand. Tiled counter is handy landing pad for hot pots and ovenware.

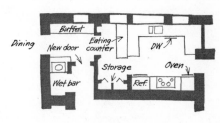

RAISED eating counter with hardwood surface partially hides kitchen clutter from dining room. It doubles as writing, telephoning desk.

Index

PHOTOGRAPHERS

Ernest Braun: 27 bottom left; 30 bottom right; 62; 63. **Glenn M. Christiansen:** 10 top; 11 bottom left; 12 top, center, bottom right; 23 top left; 29 top right, bottom; 32; 33; 42; 43 center left, bottom right; 52; 53; 66; 67 top left, top right, bottom; 68; 69; 70; 71; 76; 77; 80; 81; 82; 83; 86; 87; 92; 94; 95. **Richard Fish:** 14 top left; 15 top left; 24 bottom right; 25 top right; 27 bottom right; 29 top left; 48; 49; 56; 57; 85. **Edmund Y. Lee:** 22 bottom right. **Ells Marugg:** 4; 20 bottom right; 22 top left; 28 bottom left, right; 34; 35; 36; 37; 46; 47; 50; 51; 60; 61; 74; 75; 78; 79. **Don Normark:** 10 bottom left; 11 top, bottom right; 12 bottom left; 13 top; 14 top right, bottom left, right; 15 top right, bottom; 16 top left; 20 top; 21 bottom left, right; 22 top right, bottom left; 23 top right; 24 top; 25 top left; 26 top left, bottom; 27 top left, right; 30 top; 31 top left; 58; 59; 64; 65; 73. **Norman A. Plate:** 8 top left; 45; 88; 89; 93. **Ricco-Mazzuchi:** 30 bottom left; 43 top, bottom left. **Martha Rosman:** 8 top right; 20 bottom left; 21 top right; 24 bottom right; 26 top right; 28 top left, right. **Darrow M. Watt:** 8 bottom; 9; 10 bottom right; 13 bottom; 16 top right; 21 top left; 25 bottom left; 31 top right, bottom left, right; 38; 39; 40; 41; 44; 54; 55; 67 top center; 72; 84; 90; 91. **R. Wenkam:** 25 bottom right. **Wenkam/Salbosa:** 23 bottom left, right.